Healthy Fractions

Develop Understanding of Fractions and Numbers

Kadeem Jones

ROSEN
COMMON CORE MATH
READERS

Rosen
Classroom™

New York

Published in 2015 by The Rosen Publishing Group, Inc.
29 East 21st Street, New York, NY 10010

Book Design: Mickey Harmon

Photo Credits: Cover Dmytro Mykhailov/Shutterstock.com; pp. 3, 4, 6, 8, 10, 12, 14, 16, 18, 20, 22–24 (background) Panna Studio/Shutterstock.com; p. 5 Elena Elisseeva/Shutterstock.com; p. 7 S-F/Shutterstock.com; p. 9 (fruit salad) Markus Mainka/Shutterstock.com; p. 9 (peas) Wonderwall/Shutterstock.com; p. 11 MSPhotographic/Shutterstock.com; p. 13 Jupiterimages/Photolibrary/Getty Images; p. 15 mama_mia/Shutterstock.com; p. 17 Cre8tive Images/ Shutterstock.com; p. 19 martellostudio/Shutterstock.com; p. 21 Southern Light Studios/Shutterstock.com; p. 22 Fotokostic/ Shutterstock.com.

Library of Congress Cataloging-in-Publication Data

Jones, Kadeem, author.
Healthy fractions : develop understanding of fractions and numbers / Kadeem Jones.
    pages cm. — (Math masters. Number and operations and fractions)
Includes index.
ISBN 978-1-4777-4920-3 (pbk.)
ISBN 978-1-4777-4919-7 (6-pack)
ISBN 978-1-4777-6459-6 (library binding)
1. Fractions—Juvenile literature. 2. Diet—Juvenile literature. I. Title.
QA117.J66 2015
513.2'6—dc23
                                    2014006119

Manufactured in the United States of America

CPSIA Compliance Information: Batch #WS15RC: For further information contact Rosen Publishing, New York, New York at 1-800-237-9932.

Contents

A Balanced Diet

What are some ways to stay fit and healthy? You can exercise and eat a healthy, balanced **diet**. A balanced diet means eating the right amounts of foods from different groups, such as fruits, vegetables, grains, and dairy products. Foods from different groups help different parts of your body grow healthy and strong.

You can **divide** what you eat into fractions to see if you're eating enough of the right foods. This is a fun way to practice math and learn about healthy eating habits.

A fraction has 2 parts: a numerator and a denominator.

1 ◀ numerator: number of parts taken or looked at
—
2 ◀ denominator: total number of equal parts the whole is divided into

Fruits and Vegetables

Fruits and vegetables are some of the most important parts of a balanced diet. To check that you're eating enough fruits and vegetables, see if they make up at least $\frac{1}{2}$ of your plate for each meal.

The plates on the next page are all divided into halves, but you can't compare these fractions. That's because $\frac{1}{2}$ of the first plate is smaller than $\frac{1}{2}$ of the second plate and the third plate.

You can only compare fractions when they're parts of equal wholes. If one whole circle is much larger than another whole circle, then you can't compare fractions between them. You also can't compare fractions between a whole circle and another whole shape, such as a rectangle.

Bryce fills $\frac{1}{2}$ of his dinner plate with peas and fruit salad. His sister, Gina, also puts peas and fruit salad on her plate, which is the same size and shape as Bryce's plate. Gina's fruits and vegetables make up $\frac{1}{3}$ of her plate. Who has more fruits and vegetables on their plate, Bryce or Gina?

By comparing fractions, you can see that Bryce has more fruits and vegetables. You can use the "greater than" **symbol**, >, to show that $\frac{1}{2}$ is greater than $\frac{1}{3}$.

The fractions $\frac{1}{2}$ and $\frac{1}{3}$ have the same numerator but different denominators. The more equal parts a whole is divided into, the smaller those parts will be. That's why $\frac{1}{2}$ of a whole is greater than $\frac{1}{3}$ of an equal whole.

$$\frac{1}{2} > \frac{1}{3}$$

Fruits and vegetables also make great snacks during the day. Raisins are dried grapes. They're a good snack because they're sweet but still good for your body.

Bryce's mom puts raisins into 2 cups that are the same size and shape. She fills $\frac{1}{4}$ of the first cup with raisins. She fills $\frac{1}{2}$ of the other cup. Which fraction is smaller? A rectangle divided into fourths has smaller shares than a rectangle divided into halves. So $\frac{1}{4}$ is smaller, or less, than $\frac{1}{2}$.

You can use the "less than" symbol, which is <, to write that $\frac{1}{4}$ is less than $\frac{1}{2}$.

$$\frac{1}{4} \quad < \quad \frac{1}{2}$$

Carrots are very popular vegetables. They can be cooked, or they can be eaten raw. Raw carrots are cleaned and often cut into pieces called carrot sticks.

Bryce and his friend, Russell, both have carrot sticks in their lunches. Their plates are the same size and shape. Bryce's carrots take up $\frac{1}{4}$ of his plate. Russell's carrots take up $\frac{3}{4}$ of his plate. Who has fewer carrots? Bryce has fewer carrots on his plate because $\frac{1}{4}$ is less than $\frac{3}{4}$.

When 2 fractions have the same denominator, it means both wholes are divided into the same number of equal parts. To compare these kinds of fractions, look at the numerators. The fraction with the greater numerator is the larger fraction.

$$\frac{1}{4} < \frac{3}{4}$$

13

Broccoli is another vegetable that can be eaten cooked or raw. Eating broccoli helps keep you from getting sick.

Bryce sees 2 circular plates that are the same size and are filled with pieces of broccoli. There's broccoli on $\frac{3}{5}$ of one plate and on $\frac{2}{5}$ of the other plate. Which plate has more broccoli on it? It's the plate that has $\frac{3}{5}$ filled with broccoli because $\frac{3}{5}$ is greater than $\frac{2}{5}$. You can see that by looking at pictures of the fractions.

Does it matter if the 2 plates are the same size and shape? Yes, it does. You can only compare fractions if they're fractions of wholes that are the same size.

$$\frac{3}{5} > \frac{2}{5}$$

Great Grains

Another important part of a balanced diet is food made from grains. Whole grains are the healthiest kinds of grains. Whole-grain foods are made using the entire **kernel** of a grain.

At least $\frac{1}{2}$ of the grains that a person eats should be whole-grain foods. If a person eats enough whole-grain foods to make up $\frac{1}{6}$ of the grains they eat, is that enough? By comparing fractions, you can see it's not enough because $\frac{1}{6}$ is less than $\frac{1}{2}$.

Foods in the grain group include bread, pasta, and rice.

$$\frac{1}{6} < \frac{1}{2}$$

Eating Eggs

You should also eat enough foods that are rich in **protein**, which helps build the tissues in your body and keep them healthy. Tissues are the **materials** that make up the different parts of your body, including your heart, brain, and **muscles**.

You can eat protein for breakfast by eating eggs. Bryce has a plate with eggs and strawberries on it. The eggs take up $\frac{2}{3}$ of the plate, and the strawberries take up $\frac{1}{3}$ of the plate. Which fraction is larger?

Chicken, fish, and peanut butter are other foods that are rich in protein.

$$\frac{2}{3} \; ? \; \frac{1}{3}$$

Made from Milk

Do you like to eat yogurt, cheese, or ice cream? If you do, then you're already eating food from another important food group—dairy products. Milk and foods that are made from milk help build strong bones, muscles, and teeth.

Pieces of cheese can often be shaped like rectangles. Bryce has 2 pieces of cheese that are both rectangles. He eats $\frac{2}{5}$ of one piece and $\frac{2}{7}$ of another. Which fraction is larger? How can you show it using pictures and symbols?

How can you tell which fraction is larger? Is it important that the rectangles are the same size?

$$\frac{2}{5} \; ? \; \frac{2}{7}$$

Staying Healthy

It's fun to make healthy meals. Helping adults cook is a good way to make sure you're eating a balanced diet. Cooking is also a fun way to practice comparing fractions. Healthy food can be very tasty, and it's important to eat things that are going to help your body stay in good shape.

Exercising is another way to help keep your body healthy. Playing outside or practicing a sport is a fun way to exercise. You can even eat a healthy snack when you're done!

Glossary

diet (DY-uht) The food and drink that a person takes in.

divide (duh-VYD) To break into parts or shares.

kernel (KUHR-nuhl) A whole grain or seed of a cereal, such as wheat or corn.

material (muh-TIHR-ee-uhl) Something from which something else can be made.

muscle (MUH-suhl) A part of the body that produces motion.

protein (PROH-teen) A substance supplied by food that helps build and repair tissues in the body.

symbol (SIHM-buhl) Something that stands for something else.

Index

Due to the changing nature of Internet links, The Rosen Publishing Group, Inc., has developed an online list of websites related to the subject of this book. This site is updated regularly. Please use this link to access the list: www.powerkidslinks.com/mm/nof/heaf